Creepy, Kooky Science

Real-Life Zombies

John A. Torres

Enslow Publishing
101 W. 23rd Street
Suite 240
New York, NY 10011
USA

enslow.com

Published in 2020 by Enslow Publishing, LLC.
101 W. 23rd Street, Suite 240, New York, NY 10011

Copyright © 2020 by Enslow Publishing, LLC

All rights reserved.

No part of this book may be reproduced by any means without the written permission of the publisher.

Library of Congress Cataloging-in-Publication Data
Names: Torres, John Albert, author.
Title: Real-life zombies / John A. Torres.
Description: New York : Enslow Publishing, 2020. | Series: Creepy, kooky
   science | Includes bibliographical references and index.
Identifiers: LCCN 2019011451 | ISBN 9781978513907 (library bound) | ISBN
   9781978513891 (pbk.)
Subjects: LCSH: Parasites--Behavior--Juvenile literature. |
   Parasitism--Juvenile literature. | Animal behavior--Juvenile literature.
Classification: LCC QL757 .T66 2019 | DDC 591.6/5--dc23
LC record available at https://lccn.loc.gov/2019011451

Printed in the United States of America

To Our Readers: We have done our best to make sure all websites in this book were active and appropriate when we went to press. However, the author and the publisher have no control over and assume no liability for the material available on those websites or on any websites they may link to. Any comments or suggestions can be sent by email to customerservice@enslow.com.

Photo Credits: Real Life Zombies – Photo research by Bruce Donnola

Cover, p. 1 Borkin Vadim/Alamy Stock Photo; p. 5 Borkin Vadim/Shutterstock.com; p. 8 Mireille Vautier/Alamy Stock Photo; p. 9 ZayacSK/Shutterstock.com; p. 10 © AP Images; p. 13 Thailand Wildlife/Alamy Stock Photo; p. 15 Neil Bromhall/Shutterstock.com; p. 19 decade3d anatomy online/Shutterstock.com; p. 20 Science Source; p. 22 Everett Collection, Inc./Alamy Stock Photo; p. 25 Photo Fun/Shutterstock.com; p. 27 Frans Lanting Studio/Alamy Stock Photo; p. 30 irisphoto1/Shutterstock.com; p. 31 Agence Photographique BSIP/Corbis Documentary/Getty Images; p. 37 Diptendu Dutta/AFP/Getty Images

Contents

	Introduction	4
1	Chemicals That Can Create Zombies	7
2	Zombies of the Insect World	13
3	Rabies: The Inspiration Behind Modern Zombies	18
4	Armored Zombified Critters	24
5	Walking Corpse Syndrome	29
6	Other Diseases That Make You Feel (or Look) Like a Zombie	34
	Chapter Notes	40
	Glossary	46
	Further Reading	47
	Index	48

Introduction

Some say the fascination with zombies can be traced back to a black-and-white film from 1968 by George Romero called *Night of the Living Dead*. The dead were no longer staying buried; instead, they were mindlessly roaming the land looking for humans to bite and infect.

It's not uncommon to hear friends talking about what to do in the event of a zombie apocalypse. In fact, the US government's Centers for Disease Control and Prevention (CDC) has even come up with its very own zombie apocalypse preparedness guide.

The idea of zombies has existed for hundreds of years, mainly in folklore. West African slaves practicing voodoo, for example, believed that a spirit called Baron Samedi, who wore a big top hat and had a skull for a face, possessed the power to turn living people into zombies if they insulted him.[1]

But Stanford literary scholar Angela Becerra Vidergar believes people's fairly new preoccupation with zombies and the end of the world can be traced back to images of atomic bombs being

Today, people are fascinated by zombie culture and the idea of a zombie invasion.

dropped on Japan to end World War II. She says, however, that zombies are not the focal point of these movies and television shows, but rather the human desire to survive.[2]

But what exactly is a zombie? Most definitions include descriptions such as a reanimated corpse, a mindless human controlled by another, or a speechless human with no will of his or her own.

However, one might be surprised to learn that zombies do not only exist in the imagination or in television shows such as *The Walking Dead*. They exist in nature, and there are scientific explanations for most of them.

Pop culture says that zombies feed and make more zombies. Some real-life examples include organisms that have evolved to infect bodies of other creatures, control their will, and feed on them—all at the same time—in order to reproduce.[3] For instance, there exists a type of wasp that is actually capable of controlling large cockroaches and walking them around by an antenna, much like a human walks a dog on a leash.[4]

There are some diseases, such as sleeping sickness and rabies, that can bring about zombie-like symptoms and behavior. Rumors have also abounded of a "zombie potion" once used in Haiti to create mindless slaves to work the plantations, some of whom were believed to have died and were buried before climbing out of their own graves! There is also a rare malady that afflicts humans and convinces them that they are already dead and exist only as a zombie. In some cases, these people have urged family members to bury them.

When it's all said and done, the bloodthirsty zombies of television and the movies may actually seem more tame than the zombie stories happening in the real world.

CHAPTER 1

Chemicals That Can Create Zombies

Are zombies real? The answer depends on who is asked. Most people living in Haiti would answer yes. But in order to understand the phenomenon of zombies in Haiti, one must first understand a little bit about the poorest nation found today in the Western Hemisphere. Haiti, founded by slaves who revolted against their French captors, occupies one half of the Caribbean island of Hispaniola.

Haiti's Living Dead

There is a popular saying in Haiti that "90 percent of Haitians practice Christianity and 100 percent practice voodoo." Voodoo is a religion based in sorcery and witchcraft that West African slaves brought with them to the New World.

It is believed by those who practice voodoo that spirits belonging to people who die unnatural deaths, such as murder, are vulnerable to voodoo sorcerers who capture their souls and turn them into zombies. Only the most powerful sorcerers are believed to be able to turn the living into zombies as well. These zombies are then used as slave labor or to carry out wicked and illegal deeds.[1]

This painting by Haitian artist Hector Hyppolite, called *The Zombie*, shows a plantation owner using zombie slaves to work the fields for him.

CHEMICALS THAT CAN CREATE ZOMBIES

These stories have circulated for decades. But are there really zombies working the plantations in Haiti?

That's what twenty-eight-year-old Wade Davis was sent to investigate by Harvard University. Davis was pursuing his doctorate in biology. What prompted the investigation was a man named Clairvius Narcisse approaching his sister nearly twenty years after he was pronounced dead in a hospital and buried.[2]

Hospital records showed Narcisse was aching and feverish and spitting up blood before doctors at the American-led hospital pronounced him dead. An American doctor signed the death certificate. Narcisse was put into cold storage for twenty hours and then buried.[3]

He told his sister the story of how he was unable to move or speak while being buried and how a voodoo priest raised him that night and enslaved him.

Davis, who was an expert in plants, was sure the secret to making zombies had a scientific explanation and that it involved a West African plant called *Datura*, which is also known as the zombie cucumber plant. His goal was to obtain this potion or drug that supposedly created zombies and bring it back to Harvard where it could be studied. But to his surprise, after paying a voodoo priest

This beautiful white flower growing on the *Datura* plant is also called jimsonweed and the devil's trumpet for its mind-altering and potentially deadly effect if ingested.

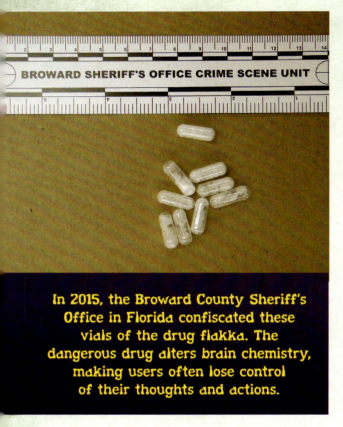

In 2015, the Broward County Sheriff's Office in Florida confiscated these vials of the drug flakka. The dangerous drug alters brain chemistry, making users often lose control of their thoughts and actions.

to make him a batch of poison used to create zombies, there was no trace of the plant at all. He was able to obtain five batches of potion to analyze.

The concoctions contained such things as ground-up toad, spiders, lizards, human bones, and other oddities. The one ingredient that all five potions had in common was a neurotoxin called tetrodotoxin, which comes from the pufferfish. This toxin, he said, can produce paralysis and a death-like state.[4]

The problem with Davis's theory is that the toxin wears off after a while. There had to be something else given to keep the victim in a zombified state for years. He believed that was where use of the plant came in. Maybe the zombie masters kept their slaves at bay by using toxins in the plant, or maybe it was just the power of suggestion brought about by the trauma of having been buried alive.

While many believe Davis solved the mystery of Haiti's zombies, there are many in the medical community who do not agree and who say many of his theories are plain wrong. Papers have also been written saying the amount of tetrodotoxin in the potions is so minute, it would have no effect at all.[5]

So, the Haitian zombie mystery remains unsolved.

More Drugs That Cause Zombie-Like Behavior

What isn't such a mystery is how other drugs, such as flakka, have made headlines for turning users into zombies. Flakka is a man-made drug sometimes known as "gravel" because it looks like aquarium gravel. It is supposed to work like cocaine, but it is much more dangerous. A small overdose of the drug can lead to violent and weird behavior.[6]

One south Florida man ripped down the hurricane-proof doors of a police station and tried to attack police officers. He admitted he was using flakka.

A Zombie Outbreak in New York

On a typical July day in Brooklyn, New York, Brian Arthur witnessed something so strange that he decided to stream it live on Facebook. There were dozens of people with blank stares stumbling around aimlessly.

He would later tell reporters that it looked like a scene from a zombie movie.[7]

Emergency personnel were called, and thirty-three people were rushed to area hospitals. They were under the influence of man-made marijuana known as K2 or "spice." The patients were slow to respond to questions and did not seem to know what was happening to them.

Further testing showed that the active ingredient that caused this bizarre incident is known as AMB-FUBINACA.

And a woman in Melbourne, Florida, who ran violently through the streets naked, proclaiming herself to be Satan, was also taking the drug.

But there has also been a lot of misinformation and hysteria regarding flakka and the abuse of bath salts, which has a similar chemical makeup to flakka.

On a Saturday afternoon in May 2012, thirty-one-year-old Rudy Eugene walked away from his job at a car wash and proceeded to attack a homeless man by biting and eating his face. The attack lasted more than eighteen minutes before police came and shot Eugene to death. The homeless man's face was nearly gone. And in the summer of 2016, a Florida State University student by the name of Austin Harrouff beat a married couple to death in their home and then proceeded to also eat the man's face.

Police announced in both cases that the men had taken the drug flakka or bath salts. The government called it an epidemic and steps were taken to limit the amounts of bath salt sales. But it turns out that toxicology tests on both men showed that neither had traces of synthetic cathinones—the chemical stimulant in flakka and bath salts—in their systems.[8]

To this day, those cannibal attacks and others like them have gone unexplained.

CHAPTER 2

Zombies of the Insect World

Zombies are not solely a human phenomenon. There are examples of zombies, mind control, and total domination in the animal world as well. But insects are some of the best zombies—and zombie makers—on Earth!

Zombie Ants

Perhaps the most horrific example of zombie-making in the bug world happens to an insect by a fungus of the genus *Ophiocordyceps*. This fungus actually needs ants to complete its life cycle.[1]

A helpless ant that was victimized by the *Ophiocordyceps* fungus mindlessly clamped down on a leaf and died while the fungus grew inside the insect and burst out of its head.

14   REAL-LIFE ZOMBIES

And not just any old ant will do. The fungus waits and knows when the right species of ant is near. Then, while the ant is foraging, the fungus infects the ant and releases chemicals that take over the ant's nervous system.[2]

The ant is no longer in control of its own body and no longer has free will at all. What happens next sounds like it's torn straight from the pages of science fiction.

Once it is infected, the ant will mindlessly climb a piece of vegetation as directed by the fungus. It will then clamp down on the plant, twig, or blade of grass and wait to die.[3] The fungus then grows a stalk right through the ant's back in order to release more of its spores on unsuspecting ants down below, starting the cycle of life and death all over again.

Scientists who discovered the "zombie ants" studied the fungus and how it affected different species of ants and found that it was able to control only one specific type of ant. In fact, the fungus produced a different type of poison or infection for each species of ant, but only one was able to be controlled.[4] One scientist theorized that perhaps there exists a fungus for every living creature that can control it.[5]

Other life-forms intent on creating zombies are a lot less subtle, such as the worm that can live inside a grasshopper and force it to jump into a body of water and drown. Some are less deadly. One fungus, for example, is capable of changing the sex of Asian tree frogs.

The Cockroach-Controlling Jewel Wasp

Wasp stings can be awfully painful. Unlike a bee, which loses its stinger once it jabs something, wasps can use theirs over and over. And some species of wasps have taken this particular feature to wreak havoc on other unsuspecting creatures to create zombies. Many wasps create zombie hosts for their larvae to feed on. But the most well-known is the jewel wasp.

The colorful jewel wasp emerges from a zombified cockroach that became a living source of food for the wasp as it matured.

Crypt-Keeper Wasp

There exists a wasp with zombie-making skills so ghastly that is was actually named after the Egyptian god of chaos and evil, Set. The wasp, *Euderus set*, behaves so much like the god of Egyptian folklore that it has become known as the "crypt-keeper wasp."[6] The god Set was said to have trapped his own brother in a crypt, where he killed and mutilated him.[7] This wasp lays its eggs in the nest of another wasp, where its larvae will eventually burrow inside the other wasp and force the host wasp to burrow a hole out of the nest. The hole is too small for the host wasp to crawl through, so the "crypt-keeper wasp" then burrows right through the other wasp to freedom.

This colorful insect hunts for large cockroaches to attack. The first thing it does is sting the cockroach in its abdomen to prevent the cockroach from being able to use its front legs. The second sting is a shot right into the roach's brain, where it also starts to pump in a venom that causes the roach to act sleepy and goofy.[8]

The cockroach shows no desire to want to escape the wasp's clutches. Instead, the roach spends about thirty minutes mindlessly cleaning itself while the wasp seeks out a burrow to use as a nest.

Exhausted upon return, the wasp breaks one of the cockroach's antennae in half and drinks the blood inside for nourishment. Then, the wasp takes hold of the rest of the antennae and leads the roach around like a person walking their dog.[9]

The cockroach mindlessly allows itself to be led to the wasp's nest. There, the wasp flips the cockroach onto its back and lays a single egg on its belly. The wasp then seals the nest.[10]

A newly hatched larva feeds on the cockroach from the inside out while it grows into a wasp. Finally, when full-grown, it burrows its way out of the cockroach, leaving just an empty carcass behind. What makes this even more horrific is that the cockroach remains alive throughout the entire process until it has been fully consumed. If the cockroach was to die, then the wasp larva would not survive.

But how does this happen? The cockroach is oftentimes much bigger than the wasp. And how does the wasp keep the cockroach alive as it's being eaten to death?

Scientists have done extensive research and have learned that the jewel wasp has perfected its stinging technique to find the tiny part of the roach's brain to target with its venom. The venom may work the same way dopamine works in humans. Dopamine is a chemical the brain releases that makes people feel good. But the wasp's venom is even more advanced than that. It works to slow down the cockroach's metabolism, meaning that it needs less oxygen and food to survive. Scientists have yet to figure out how the venom helps keep the cockroach hydrated. Some think that it's the wasp larva that accomplishes that feat.[11]

CHAPTER 3

Rabies: The Inspiration Behind Modern Zombies

Some of the most popular and terrifying scary movies over the years have dealt with vampires or zombies. The bloodthirsty vampires and flesh-eating zombies are the stuff of nightmares. But what's even scarier is that both vampires and zombies have a lot in common with a real-life disease: rabies.[1]

Rabies is a highly infectious and almost always fatal disease that is spread mainly through the bite of an animal with rabies. It is a virus that moves quickly from the infected bitten area to the brain. Rabies victims experience many symptoms, including seizures, spasms, hallucinations, and then violent or aggressive behavior.

RABIES: THE INSPIRATION BEHIND MODERN ZOMBIES

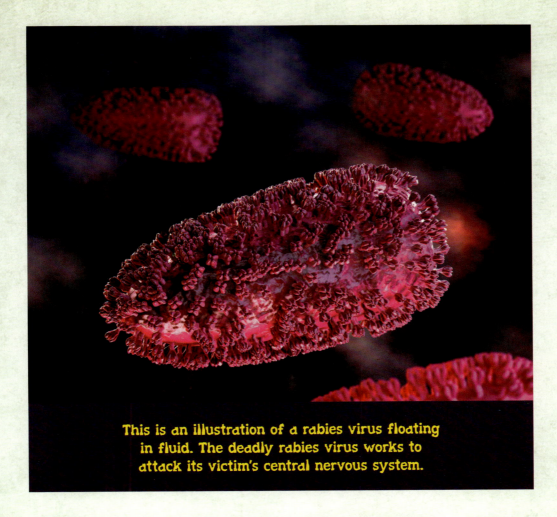

This is an illustration of a rabies virus floating in fluid. The deadly rabies virus works to attack its victim's central nervous system.

Samita Andreansky, a virologist (a person who studies viruses) at the University of Miami's Miller School of Medicine in Florida, described rabies as a virus that attacks a person's central nervous system and "can drive people to be violently mad."[2]

But that's not how it starts. In fact, someone infected with rabies may not even know it right away. The earliest symptoms are no different from other common illnesses, such as the flu, strep throat, or an ear infection. At first, the infected person will have a fever, headache, and maybe some aches and pains. But as the disease starts taking hold in someone's brain, things begin to get much worse. The person may have trouble sleeping, seem confused, have a hard time swallowing, and start producing an awful lot of saliva. In some cases, the person is even afraid of water. When these symptoms begin to show themselves, it is often too late for the infected person to survive.

Luckily for humans, the overwhelming number of rabies cases every year occur in the wild. Raccoons, skunks, bats, and foxes are the most likely creatures to be infected with rabies.[3]

Vampires, according to legend, wander at night and attack people. People with rabies often cannot sleep and become violent. Zombies are usually shown as acting like animals infected with rabies, or rabid animals: they salivate, hobble around, and sometimes wander aimlessly. Also, the disease—much like zombie infections—are spread by being bitten by an infected animal.[4]

An 1800 engraving depicts a dog with rabies. The telling signs of the illness are the mangy fur, the inability to control saliva, and the tongue hanging down from its mouth.

The Sad Numbers

What's sad is that, according to the CDC, no one has to die when bitten by an infected animal. The disease is 100 percent preventable and 100 percent curable if treated right away.

The CDC reports, however, that one person dies of rabies every ten minutes. The overall number of people killed by rabies every year is more than fifty-five thousand people, most of them living in poorer, rural sections of Africa and Asia, where the people don't have access to doctors or medicine.

The vast majority of people that become infected with rabies, especially young children, catch it from a dog bite.[5]

Is a Rabies-Zombie Apocalypse Possible?

While new strains of mutations are developing and being discovered all the time—including a new strain of rabies discovered in a New Mexico fox in 2015—many have wondered if a worldwide rabies pandemic is possible and if that is how the zombie apocalypse may begin.

Since rabies is spread only through contact with an infected animal, mainly a bite, there is no way for the disease to spread fast enough for a worldwide panic. Also, many countries, including the United States, regularly vaccinate pets, especially dogs, against rabies. It would certainly have to be a new strain to develop a resistance against vaccines.

Infectious Entertainment

Patients suffering from rabies can become so violent and so incoherent that many monsters from literature and the movies seem to be based partly on the disease.

One of the earliest references was in the classic Greek poem *The Iliad* by Homer. In it, the Trojan warrior Hector is taken over by a spirit of murderous rage that the Greeks called Lyssa. This is the same word used to describe rabies in medical books.[6]

Werewolves, vampires, and zombies are all said to have drawn some inspiration from rabies. In the 2003 horror film *28 Days Later*, director Danny Boyle said the contagious disease that turned people into bloodthirsty, violent monsters was based on Ebola and rabies.[7]

But what if somehow the disease became airborne, like the flu?[8]

That would certainly be catastrophic and possible, but highly unlikely, according to Elankumaran Subbiah, a virologist at Virginia Tech. Subbiah said that unrelated viruses, such as rabies and the flu, simply do not merge and form a new hybrid. They are so different that they would never even borrow each other's traits because they do not share the same genetic information.[9]

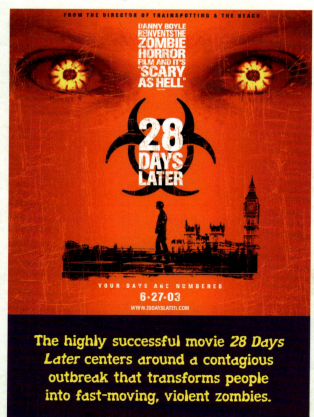

The highly successful movie *28 Days Later* centers around a contagious outbreak that transforms people into fast-moving, violent zombies.

The bottom line is that a person living in the United States is unlikely to ever get rabies, especially if he or she takes precautions when handling wildlife. But that doesn't mean it can't happen. In late 2018, a fifty-five-year-old Utah man was hospitalized for weeks before dying of the disease. No one knew he had rabies until after he died.

The man, Gary Giles, became the first person in Utah to die from rabies since 1944. His wife said they would often catch bats in their home and release them into the wild. She said they never knew that bats can carry rabies. Both she and her husband would like it when the bats would lick their fingers as they carried them outside. Her husband either contracted rabies from a bite he never felt or from being licked by an infected bat.[10]

The CDC says humans should never handle or go near raccoons, bats, foxes, or skunks.

CHAPTER 4

Armored Zombified Critters

In the wild, an animal can have its mind taken over so that it forgets what kind of animal it is. Even worse, it starts to raise the babies of another type of animal altogether. In another scary situation, an animal can be forced to imitate another animal so that birds swoop down and eat it.

While it sounds a lot like science fiction, the truth is these incredible things happen every day in nature. Some creatures carry shells on their backs mainly for protection against predators. But for some shelled animals, there is no protection against the nightmare of being turned into a zombie.

ARMORED ZOMBIFIED CRITTERS

An infected amber snail can do nothing as the parasitic worm *Leucochloridium* takes over its body and emerges from the snail's eye sockets.

Mind Control

One such example is the amber snail. This slow-moving creature is often the target of a parasitic worm known as the *Leucochloridium*. This invader enters the snail as an egg hiding in the bird poop the amber snail likes to eat.[1]

The eggs hatch inside the snail's body and start spreading out like many tentacles throughout the snail. They keep spreading out, absorbing nutrients through the snail's skin from whatever the snail eats. Then, the tentacles reach the snail's eye stalk and the real

Zombie Squid?

A 2010 YouTube video appeared to show people at a Japanese restaurant eating a squid while it danced and moved on their plates. It went viral and caused animal activists to start protest campaigns. But things are not always as they appear.

First, it was not a squid but a cuttlefish. Second, the cuttlefish was indeed dead when it was put on a plate for hungry patrons. So, is it a zombie cuttlefish? Not exactly.

The dead animal still had electrical impulses traveling through its muscles and those impulses got stronger when soy sauce or other salty items were poured on top of it. The result was that the cuttlefish appeared to have come back to life.[2]

horror begins. The worm develops brood sacs, or egg sacs, in the snail's eyes.[3]

While the worm is inside of the snail, it is totally in control. The worm does not permit the snail to breed with any other snails. It also forces the snail out of the shadows into the sunlight, which snails normally try to avoid. Finally, the worm then forces the snail to extend its eye stalks and move them around in a weird dance. They become colorful and even pulsate wildly. The movement is meant to look like two caterpillars fighting. This is known in science as aggressive mimicry. This is when an organism pretends to be another in order to lure prey to eat or to get itself eaten.[4]

In this case, the worm's goal is to attract a bird to the snail's eyes and get the bird to eat them, thinking they are caterpillars. The worm breeds inside the bird and releases its eggs into the bird's poop and starts the entire life cycle all over again.[5]

This close-up photograph shows barnacles and sea lice living on the skin of a whale.

From King Crab to Queen Crab?

King crabs, roaming the bottom of the ocean near Alaska and in the Bering Sea in search of food, can look very fearsome with their hard, spiny shells and long legs. But there is one creature that knows just how to tame the beast. It's a type of barnacle. Like snails and crabs, barnacles wear shells to protect themselves from predators. They usually live on rocks or on the bottom of ships or even on large ocean-dwellers such as whales.

But there is one type of parasitic barnacle that has decided it prefers to have its eggs looked after by a king crab rather than do it itself. Research is still new, and scientists have not figured out yet just how the barnacle parasite infects the crab. In fact, associate professor at the University of Alaska Sarah Hardy says that they have no idea how it happens. Hardy has made studying the parasite and the crab her life's work. She believes the parasite injects its cells directly into the crab's bloodstream and that allows it to eventually control the crab's brain.[6]

What is known, however, is what the barnacle parasite does to the crab. First, it begins to grow within the crab's body. It spreads and grows through very fine tentacles, and some scientists have said it resembles the roots of a plant.[7]

That is just the beginning. The parasite keeps the crab from breeding and even tricks the males into thinking they are female crabs. Hardy believes the barnacle parasite does this by affecting the crab's hormones.[8]

Then the parasite reproduces by creating an egg sac in the very same area where female crabs hold their own egg sacs. This tricks the crabs into thinking they are crab eggs, and so they start taking very good care of the barnacle parasite's eggs. They clean the sac and protect it.[9]

What is amazing is that the male crabs, which do not have the female flap where they hold their eggs, will still hold the barnacle egg sac there as if it were their own. They will even pulsate their bodies when it's time for the eggs to be released into the water so that the eggs can be released more evenly and have a better chance of survival.

Once the egg sac is gone, there is no way of knowing if the crab is still infected with the parasite without slicing it open and looking inside. Infected crabs will have green tendrils inside from the parasite.

CHAPTER 5

Walking Corpse Syndrome

In 2009, a man in the country of Belgium went to his local hospital and wanted to know why he had not been buried yet. The man told doctors that he had died several days earlier, and he couldn't understand why no one would bury him.

Just a year earlier in New York, a middle-aged woman begged family members to take her to the morgue. She explained that she was dead and needed to be with others like her. She wanted to be refrigerated in a morgue because she said her body had started to rot.[1]

These are but two of the numerous real-life case studies of people suffering from something called Cotard's syndrome, otherwise known as walking corpse syndrome. This is a rare mental illness where the person suffering believes they are already dead, no longer exist, or are beginning to rot.

Those suffering from Cotard's syndrome often believe they are dead and will travel to cemeteries because they think that is where they belong.

Even more fascinating is that doctors say these delusions exist in the sick person's mind side-by-side with very logical and rational thinking. For example, one man who believed he had died in a motorcycle accident was sent to South Africa by his family. He believed he had been sent to hell because it was suddenly so hot. Another woman who believed she was dead argued that she no longer needed food because the dead do not eat.[2]

Brains Shutting Down

Because Cotard's syndrome is so rare, doctors and scientists are still trying to figure out the science behind the sickness and delusions. One man, by the name of Graham, would be found every night at the cemetery because he was convinced he was dead. He had previously tried to kill himself by electrocution but survived.

When doctors scanned his brain to see if they could find anything wrong, they noticed that large parts of his brain had shut down. Sections of his frontal cortex were showing very low rates of metabolism, meaning the brain was acting as if it was asleep or had been shut off.[3]

One doctor who analyzed the brain scans said in the more than fifteen years of doing brain scans, he had never carried on a conversation with anyone whose brain looked like Graham's. He said the only other time he had seen brains like that were during operations when patients were put to sleep with anesthesia.[4]

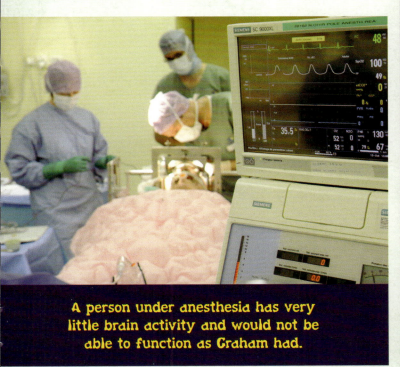

A person under anesthesia has very little brain activity and would not be able to function as Graham had.

Jules Cotard

Jules Cotard was a French doctor who specialized in the brain. He was born in 1840 and practiced medicine in Paris. After studying a patient who believed she was already dead, Cotard made his new diagnosis. Translated literally from the French, he called it "Delirium of Negation." He meant that those suffering from the illness no longer believed they existed.

Before he became a neurologist, or brain doctor, Cotard was already a psychiatrist and had also served in the military as a surgeon. His work on studying the brain was groundbreaking for his time, and he is considered to be a pioneer in the science of studying how the brain works.[5]

Stages of Walking Corpse Syndrome

Cotard's syndrome covers a wide variety of symptoms and delusions suffered by people from all walks of life. Some believe they are dead. But there have been cases of people who believe they no longer exist or have never existed. Some people believe they are immortal and can live forever. Others believe they are missing organs or body parts or were born without brains. And still others believe they have started to rot and their body parts are falling off.[6]

And while scientists are still working to try and figure it all out, one Japanese researcher by the name of Yamada Katsuragi has completed some groundbreaking work on the syndrome. He has identified three main stages of walking corpse syndrome: germination, blooming, and chronic.

Katsuragi found that it was no surprise that nearly everyone afflicted with the illness had suffered from some other mental disorders, such as psychosis or depression.

In the first stage of the disorder, germination, Katsuragi says people suffer extreme health anxiety and severe depression. He says people may start believing they are physically sick when they are not and that major organs of the body, such as the liver or heart, may be failing.[7]

The next stage, or blooming stage, is when people really start to believe they have died or no longer exist. In this stage, people stop caring about how they look or their hygiene. In the chronic stage, they can no longer do the things they would in their normal lives, such as go to work or handle chores. In extreme cases, they even stop being able to recognize family and friends or even themselves in the mirror. Also, the delusions and beliefs that they are dead become even stronger. One woman who believed she no longer needed to eat because she was dead actually starved herself to death.[8]

There is no cure for this disorder, and in the past, doctors claimed limited success by treating patients with antidepressants or antipsychotic drugs. But in recent years, scientists and doctors have begun treating the disorder with electroconvulsive therapy (ECT). This basically consists of trying to wake up the sleeping parts of the brain with small, harmless jolts of electricity.[9]

But because the disorder is so rare, there still needs to be more research done in order to find better treatment options, or even a cure.

CHAPTER 6

Other Diseases That Make You Feel (or Look) Like a Zombie

There are several other sicknesses or conditions that can cause people to behave like a zombie or even feel or look like one.

Sleeping Sickness

African trypanosomiasis is the scientific name for the illness commonly known as sleeping sickness. This disease is unique to Africa and still remains a serious health problem in some regions of sub-Saharan Africa.

OTHER DISEASES THAT MAKE YOU FEEL (OR LOOK) LIKE A ZOMBIE   35

The sickness is caused by a microscopic parasite that is transmitted by the tsetse fly. The World Health Organization (WHO) says there are ten thousand new cases in Africa every year. The illness is curable with medication, but it can be fatal if it is not treated.[1]

The problem is that many of the people infected by the parasite live in very remote and poor areas where they do not have access to doctors and hospitals. This means that they may be sick for months or years before they ever get treated.

The tsetse fly is about the size of a honey bee and bites can be very painful. If the fly is infected with the parasite, then early symptoms of sleeping sickness may start showing. Early signs are headache, achy muscles, and itchiness.

The parasite moves through the body and starts infecting the brain next. When that happens, victims become irritable, angry, and they find it hard to concentrate even on simple things. Their speech will start to become slurred and they stop eating. The main reason it is referred to as sleeping sickness is because they cannot sleep at night while finding it impossible to stay awake during the daytime. Eventually those suffering will go into a coma-like trance and can die.[2]

Sleeping sickness used to be a much bigger problem than it is today. In the early 1900s, several hundred thousand people became infected every year and many of them died. But education

Leprosy

Once one of the most feared and terrifying diseases around the world, leprosy has been brought under control with new cases being rare. More than 96 percent of the world's population is naturally immune to the disease, and in the past twenty years, more than fifteen million people have been cured of leprosy.[3]

The symptoms and disease itself are terrible. The main symptoms are skin lesions and growths that can make it look as if a person suffering with the disease is rotting away. People may also have trouble walking or fully controlling their limbs, making them walk and move like the zombies of horror movies.

regarding how to spot signs of the disease earlier, plus advancements in treatment and medication, have helped bring the disease under control. In the 1960s, sleeping sickness was nearly wiped out and numbers of those infected dipped very low. There was another major outbreak in the 1970s that took nearly twenty years to bring under control.[4]

In the past, those ill with sleeping sickness were treated with infused medications delivered through intravenous methods and combinations of other pills. But recent breakthroughs by scientists have led to the development of a single pill that many claim will cure the disease once and for all.

By 2016, there were only three thousand new cases documented, and scientists hope to wipe out the disease entirely by the year 2020.[5]

This man's hands have been destroyed by leprosy. The disease can be spread by close contact between people.

Necrosis

It's no surprise the word "necrosis" comes from the Greek word *nekrosis*, which means simply "death." Technically, necrosis is not a disease but a condition that can be caused by various other diseases or conditions, such as cancer, injury, poison, or infection.[6] But this is the condition that most closely resembles the zombies of movies and books. The images can be hard to look at: a healthy, vibrant person with an arm or a foot that is black, smelly, and starting to rot.

38   REAL-LIFE ZOMBIES

Doctors and scientists define the condition of necrosis as the "unnatural death of cells in the body." This can be caused by a lack of oxygen to a certain part of the body, an infection that goes untreated, or a harmful toxin that invades the cells. Other things that cause this condition can be extreme cold, heat, or even electricity.

An example of necrosis is when a person stranded out in freezing temperatures develops bad frostbite on his or her fingers. Eventually, the tips of the affected fingers turn black as the cells die, and the fingertips themselves have to be removed to prevent the dead cells from spreading to healthy cells.[7]

Injuries can cause necrosis as well, even something as simple as a fall from a ladder. When an area becomes injured or traumatized, blood might be prevented from flowing into the area as it normally does, carrying oxygen to the cells. Whenever this happens, necrosis is possible.

Luckily for those who do suffer an injury that may lead to necrosis, complete blood flow blockage to any area of the body is extremely painful, and so naturally the person would go to a hospital or to see a doctor. Treatment options for something like this can include antibiotics to treat the infection or surgery to get blood flowing again to the affected area.[8]

Necrosis is not contagious, meaning an outbreak is impossible. However, it is fatal if the dead cells spread their dangerous chemicals to the nearby healthy cells. Eventually, large sections become dead tissue and kill the person.

Once an area of the body is necrotic or dead, the only treatment is to remove the dead pieces. This is known as debridement. If an area is too big and too far gone, then the only option is amputation, which means cutting the dead area clean off the body.[9]

Chapter Notes

Introduction

1. Marguerite Johnson, "Curious Kids: Are Zombies Real?" The Conversation, July 11, 2017, http://theconversation.com/curious-kids-are-zombies-real-79347.

2. Kelsey Geiser, "Stanford Scholar Explains Why Zombie Fascination Is Very Much Alive," Stanford News, February 20, 2013, https://news.stanford.edu/news/2013/february/why-zombie-fascination-022013.html.

3. Kathryn Hulick, "Zombies Are Real," Science News for Students, October 27, 2016, https://www.sciencenewsforstudents.org/article/zombies-are-real.

4. Matt Simon, "Absurd Creature of the Week: The Wasp That Enslaves Cockroaches with a Sting to the Brain," *Wired*, February 28, 2014, https://www.wired.com/2014/02/absurd-creature-of-the-week-jewel-wasp/.

Chapter 1. Chemicals That Can Create Zombies

1. Brent Swancer, "The Mysterious Real Zombies of Haiti," Mysterious Universe, August 5, 2014, https://mysteriousuniverse.org/2014/08/the-mysterious-real-zombies-of-haiti/.

2. Gino Del Guercio, "From the Archives: The Secrets of Haiti's Living Dead," *Harvard Magazine*, October 31, 2017, https://www.harvardmagazine.com/2017/10/are-zombies-real.

3. Swancer.

4. Del Guercio.

5. Terrance Hines, "Zombies and Tetrodotoxin," *Skeptical Inquirer*, May/June 2008, https://www.csicop.org/si/show/zombies _and_tetrodotoxin.

6. Carina Storrs, "What Is Flakka and Why Is It More Dangerous Than Cocaine?" CNN Health, May 26, 2015, https://www.cnn.com/2015 /05/26/health/flakka-gravel-illegal-drugs/index.html.

7. Eli Rosenberg and Nate Schweber, "33 Suspected of Overdosing on Synthetic Marijuana in Brooklyn," *New York Times*, July 12, 2016, https://www.nytimes.com/2016/07/13/nyregion/k2-synthetic -marijuana-overdose-in-brooklyn.html.

8. Jacob Sullum, "The Legend of the Miami Cannibal Provides Lessons in Shoddy Drug Journalism," *Forbes*, May 5, 2016, https:// www.forbes.com/sites/jacobsullum/2016/05/05/the-legend-of-the -miami-cannabil-provides-lessons-in-shoddy-drug-journalism /#7dd285ec1a54.

Chapter 2. Zombies of the Insect World

1. Joseph Castro, "Zombie Fungus Enslaves Only Its Favorite Ant Brains," Live Science, September 9, 2014, https://www.livescience .com/47751-zombie-fungus-picky-about-ant-brains.html.

2. Castro.

3. Castro.

4. Chris Baraniuk, "Real Life Zombies That Are Stranger Than Fiction," BBC Earth, March 13, 2017, http://www.bbc.com/earth/story /20170313-real-life-zombies-that-are-stranger-than-fiction.

5. Baraniuk.

6. Jason Bittel, "New Crypt Keeper Wasp Is Parasite That Bursts from Its Host's Head," *National Geographic,* January 25, 2017, https://news.nationalgeographic.com/2017/01/crypt-keeper-wasps-parasites-new-species/.

7. Bittel.

8. Ed Yong, "The Wasp That Walks Cockroaches," *National Geographic,* June 5, 2008, https://www.nationalgeographic.com/science/phenomena/2008/06/05/the-wasp-that-walks-cockroaches/.

9. Yong.

10. Christie Wilcox, "How a Wasp Turns Cockroaches into Zombies," *Scientific American,* May 1, 2017, https://www.scientificamerican.com/article/how-a-wasp-turns-cockroaches-into-zombies1/.

11. Wilcox.

Chapter 3. Rabies: The Inspiration Behind Modern Zombies

1. Alessandra Potenza, "Were Zombies and Vampires Inspired by a Real Disease?" The Verge, October 27, 2017, https://www.theverge.com/2017/10/27/16559778/halloween-vampires-zombies-rabies-disease-legends.

2. Ker Than, "Zombie Virus Possible via Rabies-flu Hybrid?" *National Geographic,* October 27, 2010, https://news.nationalgeographic.com/news/2010/10/1001027-rabies-influenza-zombie-virus-science/.

3. "Rabies," Centers for Disease Control and Prevention, updated September 24, 2018, https://www.cdc.gov/rabies/index.html.

4. Potenza.

5. "Rabies."

6. Potenza.

7. Sandy Hunter, "28 Days Later: An Interview with Danny Boyle," Scraps from the Loft, June 5, 2017, https://scrapsfromtheloft .com/2017/06/05/28-days-later-an-interview-with-danny-boyle-2003/.

8. Than.

9. Than.

10. Tamar Lapin, "Utah Man Is State's First Rabies Death in 74 Years," *New York Post*, November 9, 2018, https://nypost.com/2018/11/09 /utah-man-is-states-first-rabies-death-in-74-years/.

Chapter 4. Armored Zombified Critters

1. Steph, "Real-life Zombies: 10 Examples of Mind Control in Nature," Momtastic Web Ecoist, 2018, https://www.momtastic.com /webecoist/2012/02/13/real-life-zombies-10-examples-of-mind -control-in-nature/2/.

2. Matt Simon, "Absurd Creature of the Week: The Parasitic Worm That Turns Snails into Disco Zombies," *Wired*, September 19, 2014, https://www.wired.com/2014/09/absurd-creature-of-the-week -disco-worm/.

3. Sarah Tse, "Nature's Zombies: Mind-Altering Infections from Snails to Humans," The Science Explorer, September 23, 2015, http:// thescienceexplorer.com/nature/natures-zombies-mind-altering -infections-snails-humans.

4. Simon.

5. Robert Shrader, "Is Japan's Cruelest Seafood Dish Actually Cruel?" Trip Savvy, December 30, 2018, https://www.tripsavvy.com /is-japans-cruelest-seafood-dish-actually-cruel-3498966.

44 **REAL-LIFE ZOMBIES**

6. Lauren Frisch, "Zombie-Generating Crab Parasites Pose Intriguing Mysteries," University of Alaska Fairbanks News and Information, March 11, 2016, https://news.uaf.edu/zombie-generating -parasites-pose-intriguing-mysteries-researchers/.
7. Leila Kheiry, "Zombie Crabs: Barnacle Infects King Crab Populations," Alaska Public Media, April 25, 2016, https://www .alaskapublic.org/2016/04/25/zombie-crabs-barnacle-infects-king -crab-populations/.
8. Kheiry.
9. Frisch.

Chapter 5. Walking Corpse Syndrome

1. Dale Hartley, "Walking Corpse Syndrome: Dawn of the Living Dead," *Psychology Today*, May 30, 2016, https://www.psychologytoday .com/us/blog/machiavellians-gulling-the-rubes/201605 /walking-corpse-syndrome-dawn-the-living-dead.
2. Hartley.
3. Rose Eveleth, "The Brains of People with Walking Corpse Syndrome May Actually be Shutting Down," *Smithsonian Magazine*, August 2, 2013, https://www.smithsonianmag.com/smart-news /the-brains-of-people-with-walking-corpse-syndrome-might-actually -be-shutting-down-22544104/.
4. Eveleth.
5. J. Pearn and C. Gardner-Thorpe, "Jules Cotard: His Life and the Unique Syndrome Which Bears His Name," *Neurology* 58, no. 9 (May 14, 2002), https://n.neurology.org/content/58/9/1400.

6. Jaleesa Baulkman, "Dead Alive: Rare Walking Corpse Syndrome Makes People Believe They Are Dead," Medical Daily, May 26, 2016, https://www.medicaldaily.com/walking-corpse-syndrome -cotards-syndrome-mental-illness-387623.
7. Baulkman.
8. Baulkman.
9. Baulkman.

Chapter 6. Other Diseases That Make You Feel (or Look) Like a Zombie

1. "Parasites: Sleeping Sickness," Centers for Disease Control and Prevention, updated May 24, 2016, https://www.cdc.gov/parasites /sleepingsickness/index.html.
2. "The Disease That Makes People Zombies," BBC News, July 15, 2005, http://news.bbc.co.uk/2/hi/health/4683903.stm.
3. Alasdair Wilkins, "5 Real Diseases That Could Make You Act Like a Zombie," IO9, June 4, 2010, https://io9.gizmodo.com/5-real -diseases-that-could-make-you-act-just-like-a-zom-5547673.
4. Melissa Hogenboom, "A Bite from This Fly Puts You into a Deadly Sleep," BBC News, December 16, 2016, http://www.bbc.com/earth /story/20161216-a-bite-from-this-fly-puts-you-into-a-deadly-sleep.
5. Hogenboom.
6. Wilkins.
7. Jennifer Whitlock, "Overview of Necrosis in the Human Body," Very Well Health, February 22, 2019, https://www.verywellhealth.com /what-is-necrotic-tissue-3157120.
8. Whitlock.
9. Wilkins.

Glossary

abdomen The part of an insect's body that contains the stomach.

anesthesia A drug given to people before surgery to block pain and help them sleep during the operation.

apocalypse The end of the world.

contract To get an illness by being exposed to something contagious.

forage To search for food or supplies.

frontal cortex The part of the brain that controls complex cognitive functions, such as attention, memory, consciousness, and communication.

misinformation False information usually meant to deceive someone.

morgue A place where bodies are kept before they are buried or claimed.

mutation The altering or changing of something into something new.

nutrient A substance that nourishes and is needed to sustain life.

overwhelming Very large or great in number.

phenomenon Something extraordinary or highly unusual.

pulsate To get larger and smaller through regular strong movement.

rabid Infected with rabies.

tendril A fine tentacle.

toxin A poison or venom created by a plant or animal.

virologist A scientist who studies viruses.

Further Reading

Books

Axelrod-Contrada, Joan. *Body Snatchers: Flies, Wasps and Other Creepy Crawly Zombie Makers*. Mankato, MN: Capstone Press, 2016.

Charlier, Philippe. *Zombies: An Anthropological Investigation of the Living Dead*. Gainesville, FL: University Press of Florida, 2017.

Simon, Matt. *Plight of the Living Dead: What Real-Life Zombies Reveal About Our World—and Ourselves*. New York, NY: Penguin Books, 2018.

Websites

The Biology Corner
www.biologycorner.com
Explore all of nature in this interactive and educational website.

Centers for Disease Control and Prevention
www.cdc.gov
Learn more about various diseases from all over the world and how to prevent and cure them.

Just Think Twice
www.justthinktwice.gov
Separate reality from fiction while learning about drug abuse.

Index

B

bath salts, 12

C

Centers for Disease Control and Prevention (CDC), 4, 21, 23
Cotard, Jules, 31
Cotard's syndrome (walking corpse syndrome), 29-33
"crypt-keeper wasp," 15

D

Davis, Wade, 9, 10

E

Eugene, Rudy, 12

F

flakka, 11-12

G

Giles, Gary, 23

H

Haiti, 7, 9, 10
Hardy, Sarah, 27-28

J

jewel wasp, 15-17

K

Katsuragi, Yamada, 32

L

leprosy, 36
Leucochloridium, 25-26

N

Narcisse, Clairvius, 9
necrosis, 37-39

O

Ophiocordyceps, 13-14

R

rabies, 6, 18-23

S

sleeping sickness, 6, 34-36
Subbiah, Elankumaran, 22

T

tetrodotoxin, 10, 11
28 Days Later, 22

V

voodoo, 4, 7-8